iMath
Readers

Designer Digs:
Finding Area and Surface Area

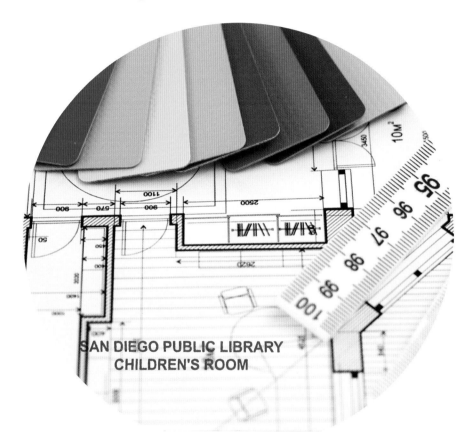

SAN DIEGO PUBLIC LIBRARY
CHILDREN'S ROOM

by Renata Brunner-Jass

Content Consultant
David T. Hughes
Mathematics Curriculum Specialist

NORWOOD HOUSE PRESS
Chicago, IL

Norwood House Press
PO Box 316598
Chicago, IL 60631

For information regarding Norwood House Press, please visit our website at
www.norwoodhousepress.com or call 866-565-2900.

Special thanks to: Heidi Doyle
Production Management: Six Red Marbles
Editors: Linda Bullock and Kendra Muntz
Printed in Heshan City, Guangdong, China. 208N—012013

Library of Congress Cataloging–in-Publication Data

Brunner-Jass, Renata.

> Designer digs: finding area, and surface area/by Renata Brunner-Jass; content
> consultant, David Hughes.
> p. cm.—(iMath)

> Audience: 10–12.
> Audience: Grade 4 to 6.

> Summary: "The mathematical concepts of perimeter, area, and surface
> area are explored as a student designs dream rooms for a school project.
> Readers learn the formulas to calculate area for quadrilaterals and triangles.
> Additional concepts include parallel lines, right angles, irregular polygons,
> decomposing shapes, and area nets. This book features a discover activity,
> history connection, and mathematical vocabulary introduction"—Provided
> by publisher.

Includes bibliographical references and index.

ISBN 978-1-59953-574-6 (library edition: alk. paper)
ISBN 978-1-60357-543-0 (ebook) 1. Geometry—Juvenile literature. I. Title.

QA445.5.B785 2012
516'.154—dc23
2012035768

CONTENTS

Note to Caregivers:

Throughout this book, many questions are posed to the reader. Some are open-ended and ask what the reader thinks. Discuss these questions with your child and guide him or her in thinking through the possible answers and outcomes. There are also questions posed which have a specific answer. Encourage your child to read through the text to determine the correct answer. Most importantly, encourage answers grounded in reality while also allowing imaginations to soar. Information to help support you as you share the book with your child is provided in the back in the **Additional Notes** section.

Bold words are defined in the glossary in the back of the book.

A Project by Design

Hi! My name is Anela. I'm going to tell you about a great project we did at school. It was a combined project for our design and math classes. Our design teacher is Mr. Li. The idea for the project was his, but we couldn't have done it without the help of our math teacher, Ms. Garcia.

Each student involved in the project drew one room of his or her home and made as many measurements as possible. We also described a design theme for each room. The theme was borrowed from something we saw in a magazine or something we wanted for a dream room of our own.

The teachers copied our drawings and descriptions. They created sets of five different rooms, and put each set into a separate envelope. Then, Mr. Li distributed the envelopes randomly to his design students. Our goal was to use the rooms and themes we received to create "designer digs." "Digs" is a slang word meaning "the place where a person lives." Mr. Li encouraged us to dream big, but also to think about ways people could realistically create the rooms we designed.

How Much Area?

All of the designs included measurements. But sometimes we needed more information. For example, we often had to find the **area**, or the total amount of space covered by a floor or a wall. To find it, we used two measurements, length and width. Area is expressed in square units.

In most rooms, the shape of the floor is a **polygon**. A polygon is a closed, flat shape with at least three sides. And all of the sides are straight lines.

Let me explain several ways you can find area.

Idea 1: Use a Grid. Let's say that a room's floor forms a **rectangle**. You can draw a model of the rectangular floor and draw a grid of squares over it.

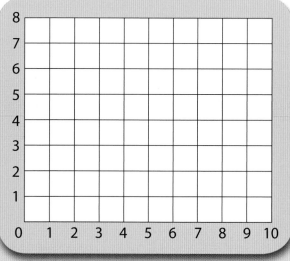

Now, let's say that each square represents a length of one foot. The floor measures 10 feet by 8 feet. So, our model rectangle is 10 units long by 8 units long.

To find the area, count the number of square units inside the rectangle. The total is expressed in square feet, or ft^2.

What is the area of the floor in the model?

Idea 2: Use a Formula. A **formula** is a mathematical rule that is written with symbols. You can use formulas to measure the area of different polygons.

Formula for Finding the Area of a Parallelogram:

A **parallelogram** is a **quadrilateral**. It has four sides, and opposite sides are **parallel**. That means the lines always remain the same distance apart. Look at these examples.

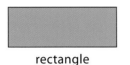

rectangle

rhombus

The formula for finding the area of a parallelogram is: $A = b \times h$

In the formula, the A stands for "area." The letter b stands for "length of the base." And the letter h stands for "height." Remember the rectangular floor described on the last page? It had a base of 10 feet and a height of 8 feet. If we use the formula, then its area is 10 feet × 8 feet = 80 square feet (ft^2).

Now, let's look at a model of another parallelogram. What is its area? Use the formula to find out.

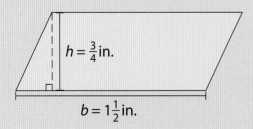

$h = \frac{3}{4}$in.

$b = 1\frac{1}{2}$in.

Formula for Finding the Area of a Triangle:

Triangles are polygons with three sides. It is useful to use a grid to examine triangles, too. Look at the example below. Each square unit on the grid represents one square foot.

The triangle's height is measured as a straight line from its base to the opposite corner. This line and the base form a **right angle**. A right angle, represented by the symbol ⌐, measures 90 degrees.

Let's use the grid to find the triangle's area. The length of the base is the **difference** between the **x-coordinates** for the **ordered pairs** (8, 1) and (2, 1) that mark the base: 8 feet − 2 feet = 6 feet. The height is the difference between the **y-coordinates** for the ordered pairs (6, 9) and (6, 1) that mark the dashed line: 9 feet − 1 foot = 8 feet.

Now you can use the formula for finding the area of a triangle: $A = \frac{1}{2}(b \times h)$.

What is the area of the triangle in square feet?

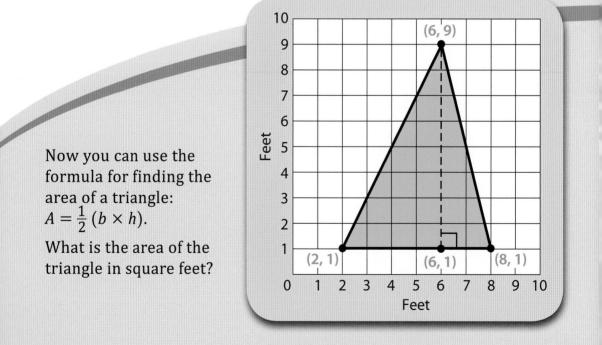

Idea 3: Decompose an Irregular Polygon. There is no formula for finding the area of an **irregular polygon**. Instead, you must **decompose**, or break apart, the irregular polygon.

For example, look at the irregular polygon below. You can draw dashed lines to show the two triangles and one rectangle inside the irregular polygon. You can find the area of these familiar shapes. Then, you can add the areas to find the area of the whole figure.

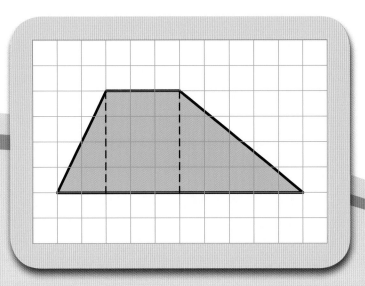

Let each grid square in the grid above represent one square inch. What is the area of the irregular polygon?

DISCOVER ACTIVITY

Materials

- tape measure, yardstick, or meter stick
- graph paper
- pencil

Think Big

Here's an exercise we did to prepare for the big math-design project. You can do it, too. Work with a partner or in a small group. Find the largest room you have access to, such as the school cafeteria or gym. If possible, choose a room with a tiled floor. For a large space in a school building, make sure to get permission to work there. Or, if weather allows and no large indoor space is available, measure an outdoor space, such as a basketball court.

Develop a plan for measuring the area of the room's floor. If the space has a tiled floor, measure the area of one tile. Multiply the measure of this tile by the total number of tiles. This will give you the area of the room. Be sure to include partial tiles in your total area calculations.

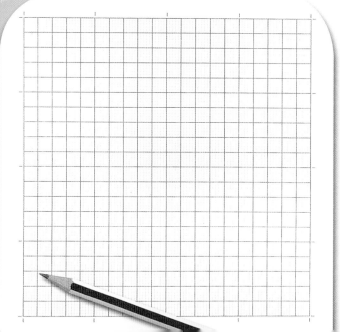

If the space does not have a tiled surface, find another way to measure and calculate the area. Use a tape measure, yardstick, or meter stick. Or use a piece of rope of a known length, and measure the width and length of the space in rope lengths. Be creative!

Draw a model of the space you are measuring on the graph paper. Let each square represent one unit of measurement for the actual space.

Decide how you will find the area of the large space. Will you:

- count grid squares?
- use a formula?
- decompose the shape into simpler shapes, and then find the area?

Choose your strategy. Then, measure and write the area of the space you measured.

Next, measure the same space using a different strategy. Compare your results.

The Colorful Square Room

Let me tell you about the five rooms I designed for this project. The first room turned out to be simplest of all. The room was a **perfect square**. And the ceiling was 8 feet high.

The student who turned in this floor plan made one particular suggestion. He or she said the room should be extraordinarily colorful. That was great news to me. I really enjoy working with color.

However, I didn't pay much attention to color at first. Instead, I made a set of black and white sketches of ideas for the room. The color could come later.

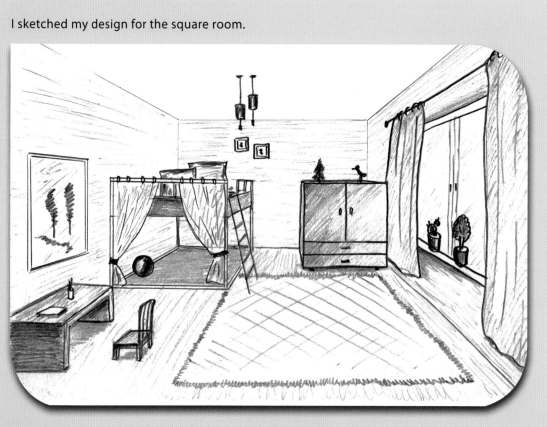

I sketched my design for the square room.

One of the few things that the person suggested was to change the closet door. It opens into the room in a way that makes it difficult to use one corner of the room. The person had written the question, "Can you think of a solution?" I thought about possible solutions for replacing this tricky door.

At the beginning of the project, we had gathered catalogs and magazines. Mr. Li guided us to some websites with more design ideas. I got an idea from a magazine. In my design, I suggested removing the closet door completely. Curtains could hang in its place. Maybe they could even be made of beads!

The curtains needed to be twice as wide as the door space and slightly longer. They should be at least 2.10 meters (m) tall and 1.5 meters wide. What area would they cover in square meters? What would the area be in square centimeters (cm)? Hint: There are 100 centimeters in one meter. So, 2.10 meters × 100 = 210 centimeters. And, 1.5 meters × 100 = 150 centimeters.

What is 210 cm × 150 cm?

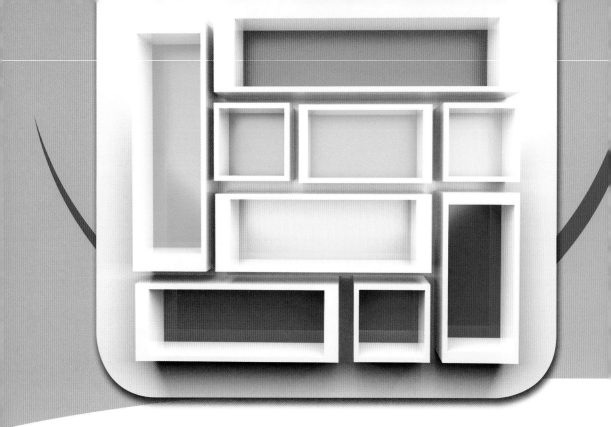

Besides color, the room's owner also enjoyed reading. The person had suggested that I design a bookshelf. I thought about different kinds of bookshelves. I didn't want to plan something ordinary.

I looked through catalogs and websites for some ideas. I liked one idea most of all. I found a way to combine color and books!

I drew a model of a collection of bookshelves. I showed how I imagined the shelves would go together on a wall. I found the **perimeter** of each shelf. Perimeter is the total distance around an object. In my model, the largest shelf measured 36 inches long and 18 inches tall.

What is the perimeter of the shelf?

Next, I thought about the floor. How could I make it more colorful? A single rug might do the job. I chose a rag rug made of strips of colorful old cloth. I used the measurements I had been given to figure out the largest rug that could fit in the room without furniture getting in the way. It could be $3\frac{1}{2}$ feet wide and $4\frac{1}{2}$ feet long.

What would the area of the rug be in square feet? What would it be in square inches? Hint: There are 12 inches in one foot. So, multiply both lengths by 12. This will be easier if each measurement is written as a decimal number first.

3.5 feet × 12 inches = 42 inches
4.5 feet × 12 inches = 54 inches
What is 42 inches × 54 inches?

I was really happy with myself when I thought about the door to the room. Doors are almost always white. Why not make it colorful, too, both inside and out?

I learned that the person who suggested this dream room would have to buy paint in certain amounts. An estimate for how much surface an amount of paint will cover is written on a can's label. So, I needed to find the surface area of the door before I could tell the room's owner how much paint to buy. **Surface area** is the total area of all the surfaces of a three-dimensional object.

First, I drew a **net** of the door. A net is a two-dimensional, or flat, shape that can be folded to form a three-dimensional, or solid, figure. The net I drew showed how the door would look if it had been cut along some edges and then flattened.

What is the surface area of the door?

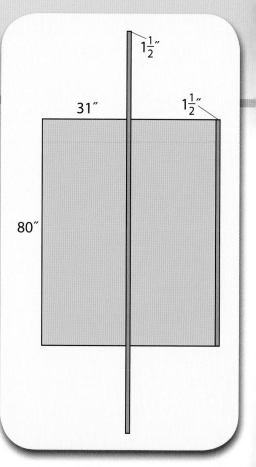

The Palace Room

I finished my plans for the colorful room and moved on to a new room. The person who suggested this room dreamed of living in a palace. I had no idea what a real palace looked like. So, I did some research. That's when an idea came to me. This could be a room in a palace in *The Arabian Nights*.

This room would be remarkable from the floor to the ceiling. I started with the floor by calculating its area. What is the area?

In my plans for this room, I included a picture of a bright blue rug. I wanted it to look like Aladdin's flying carpet.

 What's the Word?

The Arabian Nights: Tales from 1,001 Nights, a collection of fairy tales, fables, and legends, includes the story "Aladdin and the Wonderful Lamp." The stories in the collection have existed for thousands of years and are set in ancient Persia, North Africa, China, Greece, India, and Turkey.

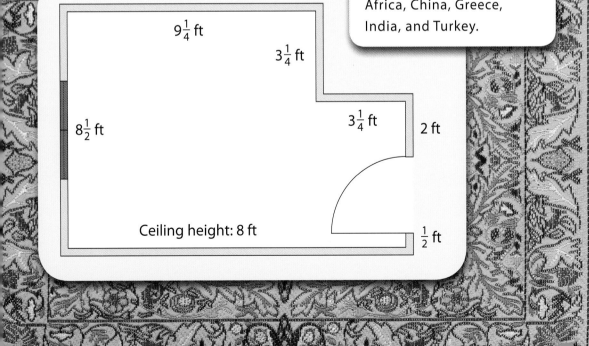

$9\frac{1}{4}$ ft

$3\frac{1}{4}$ ft

$8\frac{1}{2}$ ft

$3\frac{1}{4}$ ft

2 ft

Ceiling height: 8 ft

$\frac{1}{2}$ ft

Next, I found wallpaper that looked like the tiled walls of a Turkish palace. I suggested using the paper to cover the room's longest wall and the wall that is $9\frac{1}{4}$ feet long. What total area in square feet would be covered in wallpaper?

Topkapi Palace sits on a hill between two seas in Istanbul, Turkey.

I found pictures of rooms in different kinds of palaces. I thought they were all beautiful. There was little furniture in the ones from Arabian palaces, but it was easy to imagine sitting on large pillows scattered around the floors.

Some palace pictures showed hanging curtains around a palace bed. I liked this idea. I drew a bed like the one in another picture I had found. Perhaps someone would like the dream room I was designing and would want to build a frame for his or her bed at home. That would make it possible to hang soft curtains all the way around, creating a private hide-away.

If the frame stood 8 feet above the bed, each curtain would be 6 feet wide and 8 feet tall. There would be six curtains: one for each end of the bed and two for each side of the bed. What would be the combined area of all six curtains?

I had some more ideas for the Palace Room. One was to put something interesting on the ceiling. I wanted the ceiling to look special. So, I began by designing an eight-sided shape. I drew this diagram of it. If someone decides to use the shape in his or her real room, what area will the shape cover? (*Hint: Decompose the shape into 4 triangles and 3 rectangles.*)

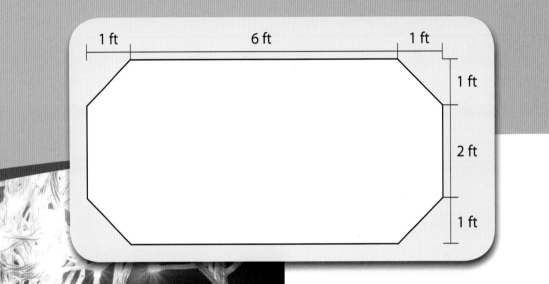

In my design, I also recommended painting the ceiling blue like a sky at twilight, just as the sun was setting. Then, someone could drape strands of lights around the ceiling like stars and imagine floating on a magic carpet above an ancient city.

I found in my research that palace rooms often have pieces of wood around the base of a wall. These pieces are called *baseboard*. Similar pieces of wood often go around the top of the walls. These pieces are called *crown molding*. Both are usually painted white. But for an Arabian palace, I had a different idea.

I suggested that a person could buy inexpensive tiles at a building store. The tiles could be glued to the wall to make an unusual baseboard.

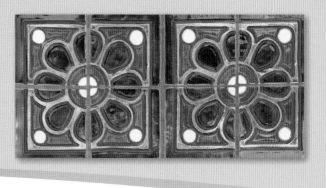

Look at the room diagram again. What is the perimeter of the floor? Do not include the door in your measurements.

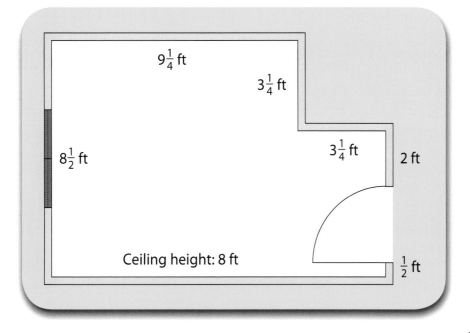

$9\frac{1}{4}$ ft

$3\frac{1}{4}$ ft

$8\frac{1}{2}$ ft

$3\frac{1}{4}$ ft

2 ft

Ceiling height: 8 ft

$\frac{1}{2}$ ft

This ancient Roman mosaic is now in a mosaic museum in Istanbul, Turkey.

CONNECTING TO HISTORY

Beginning at least 5,000 years ago, people used tile to cover floors. The tiles were arranged carefully to make **mosaics**. Mosaics are pictures or patterns made from colorful bits of hard materials.

The earliest known mosaic floors were created in ancient Mesopotamia, a region between the Tigris and Euphrates Rivers in the Middle East. Builders used colored pebbles, as well as shells and ivory. Mesopotamians also decorated stone columns with mosaic patterns.

About 2,300 years ago, the Greeks made mosaic floors in the homes of wealthy people. These Greek artists began to cut cubes of stone to use in their work. Different sizes and colors of cubes allowed the Greeks to make incredible designs.

The Greek influence traveled to Italy, the center of the Roman Empire. The Roman Empire reached from modern Britain, east to Armenia, and all along the coast of Northern Africa.

EMPIRE ROMAIN PAR A.H.Dufour.

These pieces of mosaic floor were uncovered in the Villa Romana del Casale in Sicily, Italy. The home may have once belonged to someone very important, like a member of the Roman emperor's family.

Wealthy Romans usually had a *villa*, or second home outside of main cities. Villas with mosaic floors made of thousands and sometimes more than one million tiles were built across the empire. One such villa was the Villa Romana del Casale, in Sicily. Sicily is an island that is part of modern Italy.

A landslide buried the Villa Romana del Casale 700 years ago. Being buried helped to preserve its mosaic floors. As people began to remove the dirt that had covered the building for so long, they found both private and public rooms. Such rooms suggest that the owner was likely a Roman senator, someone chosen to help run the empire.

The Tree Room

The next room I designed wasn't in a palace. It wasn't in a villa. It wasn't even in a regular house. This room was built around a tree! This might have been a real room, or perhaps it was entirely imaginary.

The person who suggested this room said that it resembled a tree house. People could relax, eat, and sleep in the house. I researched tree houses. I found some interesting examples, even one that had been built around a tree!

This room had to stay on the ground, though. I examined the room's measurements. What is the area of the Tree Room floor?

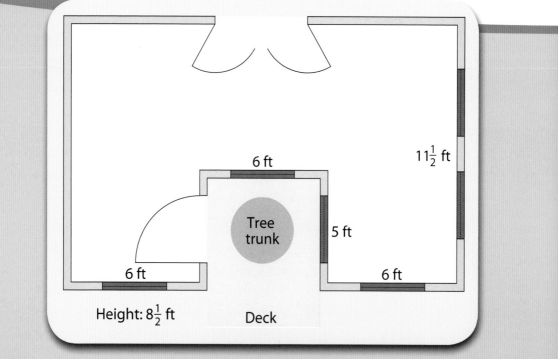

6 ft

$11\frac{1}{2}$ ft

Tree trunk

5 ft

6 ft

6 ft

Height: $8\frac{1}{2}$ ft

Deck

The person who turned in this floor plan had included pictures of the furniture in the room. There was a perfect square wooden table that measured 16 inches on each side. I had learned a lot about mosaics recently in my research for this project. So, I printed a photo I found on the Internet as an example for a colorful design for the table. I also noted that hobby stores sell bags of mosaic pieces that are ready to be glued into place.

A person would need to buy enough bags of tile to cover the table. What is the area of the table's top?

What's the Word?

The word *mosaic* comes from the same root as the word *music*. Both come from an ancient word meaning the Muses of ancient Greek mythology. In mythology, the nine Muses were women who inspired all creativity. There were muses of literature, science, and the arts.

This room had to be lively. After all, the room had been built around a living tree. I wanted the room to be colorful, full of energy. So, I decided the long wall that had the two windows would be bold yellow.

To plan for the amount of yellow paint needed, I calculated the area of the wall. It was $11\frac{1}{2}$ feet wide and $8\frac{1}{2}$ feet tall. I calculated the total area of the windows as 12 square feet.

What was the area of the wall, not including the windows?

The longest wall had the main doors to the room in it. I decided I would paint over the doors as well, so they matched the wall.

The wall to the left of the longest wall in the diagram of the room had no windows or doors.

For my design, I decided to use a second color for these two walls. What is the total area for both of these two large walls?

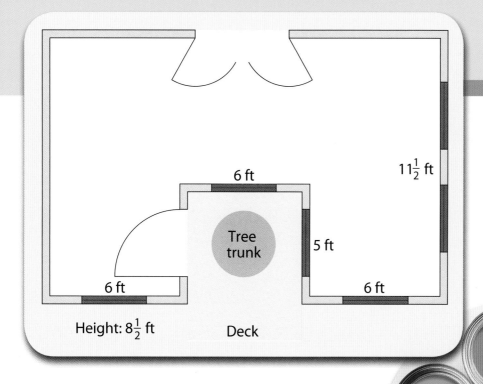

I planned to use a third color for the other five walls. I estimated the area of each one, then subtracted the areas of all the windows and the door to the deck. If this was a room in real life, it was going to take a lot of paint!

I thought about the tree that would show through so many windows. I also thought about the shade it would give the room and the bright colors I had suggested for the walls. Suddenly, I realized I might like this room for myself!

The room had no closet, and the person who drew this room suggested adding more storage space. Whether short or tall, a dresser was needed, and it should be made of wood. In my design, I recommended visiting shops that sold old furniture to anyone using this design. It would be possible to find something cheap that could be improved with a little paint and creativity.

The dresser would have to fit within in a floor space that was $1\frac{1}{2}$ feet by $4\frac{1}{2}$ feet. What is the maximum area of floor space that the dresser could fill?

I thought about the tree house. Why, I wondered, would someone build a room around a tree? I decided it was because that person enjoyed nature. So, my last suggestion was for a person using this design to build a bird feeder to put in the tree. Then, he or she could watch the birds from inside the room.

The bird feeder could be a flat wooden board. This would give the birds a place to perch while they pecked at seeds. A board at least 16 inches long and 8 inches wide should provide the birds plenty of room. What is the area of the board's surface?

An interior designer uses her strong math and artistic skills to help customers create the space they want.

MATH AT WORK

Working on this project is like being an interior designer. An interior designer is someone who decorates or remodels indoor spaces. When an interior designer begins a job, she meets with the customer first. They talk about what the customer wants.

After collecting information, the designer makes calculations. Then, she draws designs. Each design includes measurements and suggested design changes. It also includes costs for all necessary materials. The plan may also include costs for getting the job done.

The designer and customer work together and agree on a final plan. Then, the designer arranges for the project to be completed. For bigger remodeling jobs, a designer may introduce the customer to an architect or contractor. A contractor is someone who manages building and remodeling projects. The designer works with the customer and others until the project is complete.

The Basketball Room

I didn't think anything could be more fun than designing a room in a palace or a new kind of tree house. But I was wrong. The theme of my next room was to design a space for twin sisters who loved basketball. I'm a huge fan, too. So, this room was especially fun to do.

I looked closely at the diagram and notes I had been given. What is the floor's area?

There was a second drawing in the envelope. It modeled the ceiling. The ceiling gave the room an odd shape. The wall that had no windows was 10 feet high, while the opposite wall was 8 feet high. So, the ceiling was slanted.

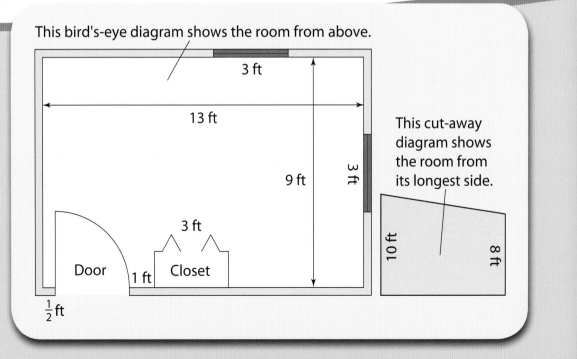

This bird's-eye diagram shows the room from above.

3 ft

13 ft

9 ft

3 ft

3 ft

Door

1 ft   Closet

$\frac{1}{2}$ ft

This cut-away diagram shows the room from its longest side.

10 ft

8 ft

When I think of basketball, the colors orange and black come to mind. I thought the room could use some color. But the room had only two windows. Dark colors on all of the walls would make the room too dark. So, I decided to paint the tallest wall and the windowless side wall orange. I included the door in my calculations.

What is the combined area of the tallest wall and the windowless side wall?

The blue area before the net is the free-throw lane.

Since the people who would share this dream room were twins, I thought it would be a good idea to divide the room in half. I thought hard about how I could do it. Finally, I settled on the idea of painting a free-throw lane in the middle of the room.

A real free-throw lane on a basketball court is 19 feet long and 12 feet wide. What is the area of an actual free-throw lane?

The room would be far too small for a real free-throw lane. So, I planned a lane $4\frac{3}{4}$ feet long and 3 feet wide. I suggested that someone could hang a net for a foam basketball on the wall at the back of the lane.

What would be the area of the free-throw lane in the Basketball Room?

I thought about the suggestions I had made so far. Two orange walls. A free-throw lane painted on the floor. A basketball hoop attached to a wall. The room practically screamed basketball!

I had one more idea in mind. I held my own basketball in my hand. I loved its tough, pebbled skin. I loved the colors, too. Two walls in my Basketball Room design were orange. But an important color was missing. So, I suggested painting a solid black line all the way around the room. The stripe, I thought, should be painted halfway up each wall. There would be no break in the line along the closet or the door, but there would be a break in the line for both windows. How long would the black stripe be?

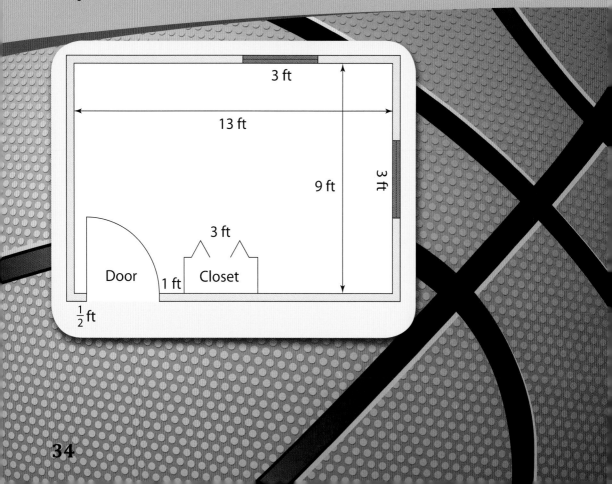

The Space Room

I called my last room design the most "far-out" of all. The student who suggested this dream room had his or her head in the stars. This was going to be the Space Room.

According to the notes that came with the room's floor plan, this dreamer was a fan of everything to do with astronomy and space travel. I did some research, and, as I worked, I came up with lots of ideas. I tried to make them possible for anyone to use.

I studied the floor plan first. The room was large with an unusual shape.

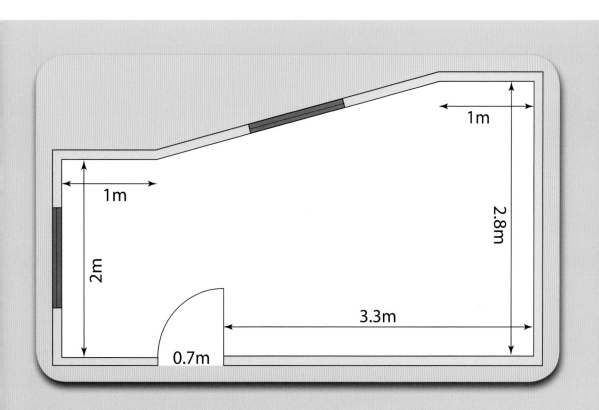

What was the area of the floor?

I thought special wallpaper would be perfect for one wall of the Space Room. I looked online and found lots of possibilities, including peel-and-stick wallpaper.

I looked at the room's floor plan. I thought the wall on the right end of the room was perfect for wallpaper, as there were no windows or doors to interrupt the space. Remembering from the notes that the ceiling was 2.4 meters high, I calculated the wall's area.

What was the area of the wall?

Astronauts aboard *Apollo 8* entered the Moon's orbit on December 24, 1968. The astronauts showed pictures of Earth and the Moon as they saw it from their spacecraft.

I continued my search online and found lots of decorating possibilities. I found space-themed towels, bedspreads, curtains, and rugs. One rug had a flattened view of Earth. Anyone using my design could walk across all seven of the planet's continents in only a few steps.

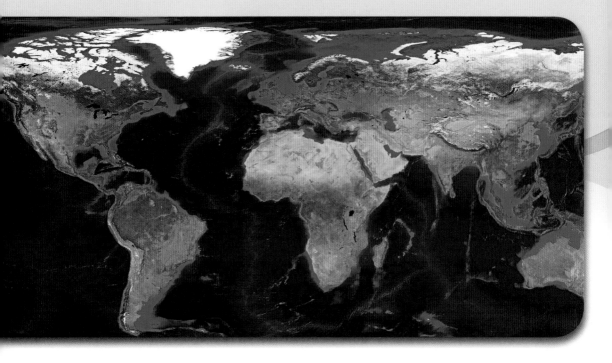

The rug measured 48 inches by 96 inches. What is its perimeter? What is its area?

I saw some white paper lanterns and thought how they might resemble glowing stars in a dark room. In my design I suggested painting the ceiling black like outer space. Then someone could hang white paper lanterns in different sizes from the dark ceiling.

Light from the lanterns could represent the light of stars in the Milky Way, our home galaxy. There may be up to 400 billion stars in the Milky Way. There isn't enough space in any room to hang nearly so many lanterns. But it would take only a few bright lights for someone to imagine the stars in the sky.

I had one more idea for the Space Room. I went online to the website for the National Aeronautics and Space Administration (NASA). They have a huge collection of photographs and posters that can be printed from a personal printer.

Designers at the Kennedy Space Center made a pair of posters for each space shuttle mission. One poster in each pair was a crew poster. It included photographs of the astronauts on the mission. The second poster was a mission poster. It described the purpose of the mission and often showed the spacecraft.

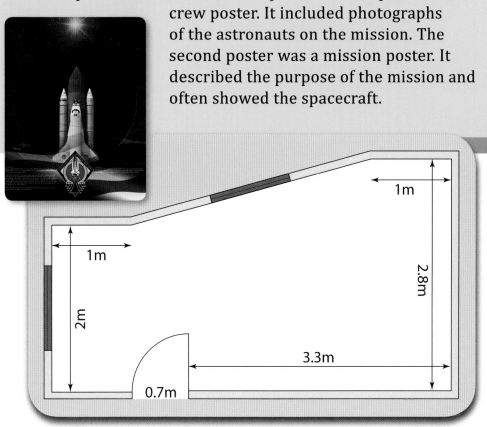

I recommended that anyone using my Space Room plan should print the crew poster for Shuttle *Atlantis*. Then, he or she could take it to a print shop to have it enlarged. I recommended hanging the poster on the wall "behind" the door—that is, to the right of the door as you walk into the room. I checked my notes again and recalled that the ceiling is 2.4 meters high. What's the largest size the poster could be?

I can't have a Space Room without spaceships, I thought. The notes that came with the room's floor plan mentioned that the student had a lot of spaceship models. They were special spaceships, though. Many were old.

The student's grandfather had been interested in space, too. So, had his great-grandfather. Both had collected space toys. The toys now belonged to the student.

The toys needed to be stored carefully but not hidden from view. So, I suggested buying lots of plastic display boxes at a hobby shop. The boxes could be hung from any wall.

I found a clear plastic box that measured 15.5 inches long, 7.5 inches wide, and 6.5 inches tall. What is the area of the base of the box?

The Big Wrap-up

At last it was time to turn in our designs. Surely, I thought, no one else had been asked to design such different rooms. The first idea had been simple. The student's dream room would be filled with color. Then, the rooms had become more unusual. I had designed a room for a palace. A new version of a tree house followed that. Then came a room dedicated to basketball. And finally, there had been a room that would allow an imaginative owner to spend time in space.

We shared our projects with each other, Ms. Garcia, and Mr. Li. We all agreed that it was surprising how one person's idea could turn into something so creative and unusual. Our next project, we agreed, would be to design a dream room of our very own. We certainly had enough ideas to inspire us.

What would your dream room look like?

I shared some design ideas for my own dream room with my parents. We talked about painted walls, wallpaper, posters, rugs, and display boxes. I have a lot of interests, including sports and space. But I enjoy nature, too, and I have a large collection of insects that are no longer living. Most of them are stored in cardboard boxes, but my parents agreed we should try to show my insect collection in display cases. We started with a few of my butterflies. They look great inside a black frame.

After putting my insect collection into cases, I realized that I had more than one specimen, or individual, of insects in my collection. My parents suggested that I send the duplicates to my cousin who also has an insect collection. We went to an office supply store and found a net for a shipping box that we could fold and put together ourselves.

I drew this model of the net for the shipping box.

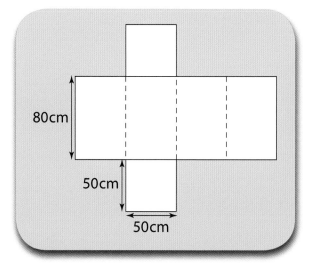

What is the surface area of the shipping box? What are some methods for finding the answer?

Idea 1: Use a Grid. I could draw grid lines on the net. But I would have to draw a lot of grid lines!

Idea 2: Use a Formula. The net is made of rectangles and squares, which are parallelograms. I can use a formula to find the area of each parallelogram in the net. Then, I can add the areas together.

My net has no triangles. So I don't need the formula for finding the area of a triangle.

Idea 3: Decompose an Irregular Polygon. My net is composed of regular polygons. Or, we could say it is already decomposed. So, it isn't necessary to decompose the shapes before calculating total area.

I decided to use the formula for finding the area of parallelograms to find the surface area of the shipping box.

The four large quadrilaterals on the net are each 80 centimeters long and 50 centimeters wide. The two small quadrilaterals are 50 centimeters long on each side.

Each large quadrilateral has an area of 80 cm × 50 cm = 4,000 cm^2.

Each small quadrilateral has an area of 50 cm × 50 cm = 2,500 cm^2.

(4 × 4,000 cm^2) + (2 × 2,500 cm^2)

What is the total surface area of the box?

There are 10,000 square centimeters in 1 square meter. So, it's possible to divide the area by 10,000 to get an answer in square meters. What is the total surface area of the box expressed in square meters (m^2)?

Now that I've sent my cousin a box and unpacked my collection, I am going to keep decorating my room with more colorful insects. I'm looking forward to living in my nature-themed dream room!

Make a drawing of a room at your home. Measure the heights and lengths of all walls. Find the area of the floor. Is the ceiling the same shape as the floor? What are the areas of any doorways and windows?

Record all of your measurements on your drawing. Then, think about ways you would like to change your room. Would it have a theme or special purpose? In other words, would the room focus on a sport, music, art, or something else you enjoy?

Create a model of your dream room. Share your model with your friends or family. They may have even more ideas to add to your own.

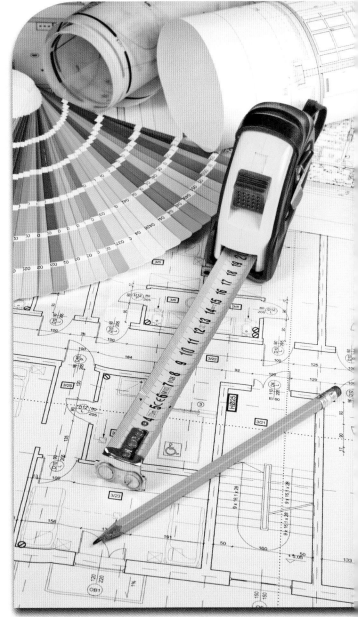

All interior designs begin with measurements.

GLOSSARY

area: the measurement of a flat, 2-dimensional surface.

decompose (a polygon): to identify and find the area of each regular polygon inside an irregular polygon in order to find the area of the entire shape.

difference: the amount left over after one number is subtracted from another.

formula: a mathematical rule written with symbols.

irregular (polygon): a polygon whose sides are not all equal in length and whose angles are not all equal in measure.

mosaic: a picture or pattern created by arranging small colored pieces of a hard material such as stone, tile, or glass.

net: a two-dimensional shape that can be folded to make a three-dimensional shape.

ordered pair: a pair of numbers that name a point on a coordinate grid.

parallel: two lines or line segments that always remain the same distance apart.

parallelogram: a quadrilateral with opposite sides that are parallel and the same length.

perfect square: a quadrilateral with four right angles and four sides that are all the same length.

perimeter: the measure of the distance around a closed shape.

polygon: a closed, flat shape with at least three sides and in which all sides are straight lines.

quadrilateral: a polygon with four sides.

rectangle: a quadrilateral with four right angles and two pairs of parallel sides.

right angle: an angle that measures exactly 90 degrees.

surface area: the *area* of all the surfaces of a three-dimensional space; usually the total area of the outside of an object.

triangle: a polygon with exactly three sides.

***x*-coordinate:** the first value that appears in an ordered pair.

***y*-coordinate:** the second value that appears in an ordered pair.

FURTHER READING

FICTION
Operation Redwood, by S. Terrell French, Amulet Books, 2009

NONFICTION
Ancient Roman Art and Architecture, by Don Nardo, Lucent Books, 2012
It's Your Room: A Decorating Guide for Real Kids, by Janice Weaver and Frieda Wishinsky, Tundra Books, 2006

ADDITIONAL NOTES

The page references below provide answers to questions asked throughout the book. Questions whose answers will vary are not addressed.

Page 6: 80 ft²

Page 7: $1\frac{1}{2}$ in. $\times \frac{3}{4}$ in. $= 1\frac{1}{8}$ in.²

Page 8: $A = \frac{1}{2}$ (6 ft × 8 ft) = 24 ft²

Page 9: 26 in.²

Page 13: 3.15m²; 210 cm × 150 cm = 31,500cm²

Page 14: $P = 108$ in.

Page 15: $15\frac{3}{4}$ ft²; 42 in. × 54 in. = 2,268 in.²

Page 16: [(80 in. × 31 in.) × 2]+ [(80 in. × $1\frac{1}{2}$ in.) × 2] + [(31 in. × $1\frac{1}{2}$ in.) × 2]= 5,293 in.²

Page 17: The room's shape can be decomposed into two rectangles: $78\frac{5}{8}$ ft² + $17\frac{1}{16}$ ft² = $95\frac{11}{16}$ ft²

Page 18: ($12\frac{1}{2}$ ft × 8 ft) + ($9\frac{1}{4}$ ft × 8 ft) = 100 ft² + 74 ft² = 174 ft²

Page 19: 6 × (6 ft × 8 ft) = 6 × 48 ft² = 288 ft²

Page 20: Possible solution:

4 triangles:
$A = [4 \times \frac{1}{2}$ (1 ft × 1 ft)] + (8 ft × 2 ft) + [2 × (6 ft × 1 ft)] = 2 ft² + 16 ft² + 12 ft² = 30 ft²

Page 21: $39\frac{1}{4}$ ft

Page 24: 177 ft²

Page 25: 256 in.²

Page 26: $85\frac{3}{4}$ ft²

Page 27: The length of the longest wall is equal to the lengths of the three wall sections opposite it in the room: 6 ft + 6 ft + 6 ft = 18 ft. The area of the two walls equals ($11\frac{1}{2}$ ft × $8\frac{1}{2}$ ft) + (18 ft × $8\frac{1}{2}$ ft) = $97\frac{3}{4}$ ft² + 153 ft² = $250\frac{3}{4}$ ft².

Page 28: $6\frac{3}{4}$ ft²

Page 29: 128 in.²

Page 31: 117 ft²

Page 32: The tallest wall has an area of 9 ft × 10 ft = 90 ft². The side wall can be decomposed into a triangle with $A = \frac{1}{2}$ (13 ft × 2 ft) and a rectangle with $A = $ 13 ft × 8 ft. The combined area is 90 ft² + 13 ft² + 104 ft² = 207 ft².

Page 33: 228 ft²; $14\frac{1}{4}$ ft²

Page 34: 38 ft

Page 35: Decompose the shape of the floor. Total $A = 1.2$ m² + 0.8 m² + 10 m² = 12 m².

Page 36: 6.72 m²

Page 37: 288 inches; 4,608 in.²

Page 39: 7.92 m²

Page 40: 116.25 in.²

Page 44: 21,000 cm²; 2.1 m²

CONTENT CONSULTANT

David T. Hughes

David is an experienced mathematics teacher, writer, presenter, and adviser. He serves as a consultant for the Partnership for Assessment of Readiness for College and Careers. David has also worked as the Senior Program Coordinator for the Charles A. Dana Center at The University of Texas at Austin and was an editor and contributor for the *Mathematics Standards in the Classroom* series.